PowerShell

The Complete Beginners Guide for Windows PowerShell. A Step by Step Guide for PowerShell Scripting!

BRAYDEN SMITH

TABLE OF CONTENTS

Introduction

Congratulations on purchasing *PowerShell* and thank you for doing so.

The following chapters will discuss everything that you need to know in order to get started with some of your own coding in the PowerShell language. This is considered one of the easiest coding languages to learn how to use, and we will take a look not only at some of the components that come with this kind of language but also some of the different codes that you can use and which will help you to see results with this language in no time at all. As we work through this guidebook, you may even be surprised at some of the results that you get, and how easy this language really is!

To start with, we are going to do a quick introduction to what PowerShell is all about and why it is one of the best languages out there to learn how to use. When we are done with that, we are going to start exploring some of the other things that you are able to do when it comes to PowerShell including getting started with some basic commands, how to handle the outputs and the pipelines, and some of the different operators and wildcards that will make a difference in the codes you write.

From there, we are going to move on to some more information on how you can do things with the PowerShell code. In this part, we are going to take a dive into some of the drives and providers that are available with PowerShell, how to work with some of the quotes and strings, how to execute the commands that you want to use, and even how you are able to do the process in the proper manner to format your data and your handle objects while creating your own tables in the process.

The end of this guidebook is going to help us to look a bit more into some of the coding that you are able to do when it comes to PowerShell and how this can help you to write out some stronger codes in the process. In these chapters, we are going to explore how you can work with some of the remote and the multitasking functions that are sometimes necessary when it comes to coding, and even how to automate an SQL server if you need.

There are so many things that you are able to do when it comes to working with PowerShell and some of the coding that is popular with this kind of language. When you are ready to learn how to work with PowerShell and what it can do for some of your programming needs, and you like to work with the Windows program, make sure to check out this guidebook to help you get started.

There are plenty of books on this subject on the market, thanks again for choosing this one! Every effort was made to ensure it is full of as much useful information as possible. Please enjoy!

Chapter 1

What is PowerShell?

The first thing that we need to take a look at here is what PowerShell is all about. The world of coding is a very exciting place. There are a lot of different types of languages out there that you are able to learn how to use, but PowerShell is one of the best ones to learn. This coding language is available through Microsoft, and it is going to be a new kind of Command Line Interface that makes it easier to use with your Windows system. If you have worked with the Windows system in the past, and you have some familiarity with this, you will find that the PowerShell is one of the best options for you to use.

To start with though, PowerShell is going to be a shell, also known as a type of interactive user interface that can work with your operating system (in this case, with the Windows operating system), that Microsoft developed in order to help the programmer deal with task automation and management of configurations. This shell is a powerful tool, and it is going to be based on a framework that is .NET. This shell is also going to come with its own command line as well as its own coding language to make sure that you can use all of the tools available to get different tasks done. PowerShell is also going to be able to come with what is known as the Windows ISE to help you create the different scripts that you need, without having to remember or type in all of the commands.

To help us get a better understanding of how PowerShell works, we first need to take a look at what the shell is all about. When we are looking at computer science, the shell is going to be the interface for the user that will give you access to a variety of services that you can use with the operating system. A shell can be based on one of two things. It can either be command-line based, or it can be based on GUI or graphical user interface.

PowerShell is going to be a shell that was developed in the beginning to help with configuration management and some task automation. But over time, the PowerShell has changed a bit, and it is now a project that is open-sourced and can be used on any kind of platform or operating system that you would like. This shell is going to be based on the framework of .NET, and it is also going to come with a scripting language and a command-line shell-like before.

This brings up the question of what you are able to do. Microsoft designed this product as a tool to help the programmer to automate and solve in a fast manner a lot of tedious administration tasks. For example, you are able to use PowerShell in order to display all of the different types of USB devices that are installed on one computer or one system of computers. You can even set up a time-consuming task so that it is able to run in the background and complete when it needs to, while you do some other work. Another option with PowerShell is that it is used to identify and kill processes that are not responding to what you are doing.

The capabilities that come with PowerShell are going to allow you to simplify and automate some of the repetitive and tedious tasks by creating some scripts and combining together multiple commands. And if you are the person who is considered the administrator of the network, the PowerShell is going to be helpful when it comes to working on Active Directory. Given that it is going to hold onto many different cmdlets, which are the customizable commands, PowerShell is going to be one of the best ways that you are going to be the most productive as you can on your system.

To make sure that things are kept as simple as possible, we can think of PowerShell as an interface for command lines that are designed to work with the Windows System. But there are going to be a lot of parts that need to come together in order to help create PowerShell and make sure that it works the way that you want. Some of these parts include:

1. Existing Windows Command line tools

2. Commands with PowerShell.

3. Functions that work with PowerShell

4. Access to the API for the .NET Framework

5. Access to the Windows Management Instrumentation

6. Access to the Dynamic Linked Libraries that are available with Windows

There are a lot of different features that you can use when you are working with PowerShell. This system is going to work well with some of the other APIs, as well as some of the other programs and more that are already on the Windows systems. This is just one of the many different reasons why PowerShell has become so popular to work with. And it is going to be included in your Windows System so you won't have to go through all of the work of downloading it or making sure that it is installed on your computer in the proper manner.

The next thing that we want to take a look at is some of the things that you are able to do with PowerShell. While it is likely that this kind of program is already going to be found on your computer if you are working with a Windows computer, you may be curious about what you are able to do with this kind of coding language. You will find that this program is going to be easy to learn and it is going to come with a ton of features that you are able to work well with the Windows System, which can help you to get things done.

In the beginning, PowerShell was developed in order to help you to automate and solve many of the tedious and oftentimes hard tasks that are present on the computer right now. For example, you can use this kind of program in order to look through the computer and see how many different USB devices are installed on all of the computers in the same network, rather than having to manually go around to each one and check.

You can use PowerShell in order to help you set up some of the tasks that take a ton of time to complete and then set them up to work in the background while you are working on your other tasks. And it is possible to use this PowerShell program in order to first find, and then shut off any of the processes that are not responding the way that you want, or filter out some of the information that is on your computer or on the chosen network before it is exported to the format of HTML.

Of course, these are just a few of the tasks that you will be able to do when you start working on PowerShell. It is possible to use this as a way to simplify and then automate some of the tasks that are available to use as an admin. This coding language can be used to create some scripts for these tasks, and then will combine together two or more commands to make sure the coding and the processing are as easy as possible.

It is possible as an administrator of the network to use PowerShell to help them deal with the Active Directory. Since PowerShell is able to hold onto a ton of commands, you will not have to waste a lot of your own time on doing these kinds of tasks in the first place. This allows PowerShell to work on the network you run, and it will make things more efficient and more productive in the long run.

To keep things simple here, you are going to make sure that you use PowerShell to make the process of running your network a lot easier, without all of the wasted energy and time that these tasks usually take. While there are other coding languages available, and they often promise the same kind of thing, none of them are going to prove as effective as the PowerShell program when it comes to getting the work done. Add to this that the program is going to work well when it is used with the Windows system, and you know this command-line interface is going to do everything that you want.

There are a lot of different benefits that you are going to enjoy when it comes to working with the PowerShell code. You can pick from a lot of other coding languages if you would like, but PowerShell is simple and has other benefits that help to put it apart from some of the others. Some of the benefits that you will be able to see when it comes to using the PowerShell program include:

1. **It is fast and easy to use.** You will find when we start doing some of the coding in this guidebook that PowerShell is an easy program to use. Many beginners like to use this to give themselves experience on how to code ad get things done on their program.

2. **Works well with the Windows system:** If your chosen operating system is Windows, then you will find that the program of PowerShell is already going to work well with it. This is a great program to use because it works with Windows, and it will give you the features and the security that you need in a coding language.

3. **Small codes:** If you have ever looked at some of the other coding languages that are out there, you may have seen long lines of code that you had to write out and learn. But with

PowerShell, your codes are just going to need a few lines, and sometimes it's as simple as a few words, in order to get the code to work for you.

4. **PowerShell is already found on your computer.** Windows has this command-line interface present on its system from the start. You can go through and download a newer version if you would like, but there is already going to be a version found on your computer to make things a bit easier.

As you can see here, there are a lot of reasons to use PowerShell and a lot of benefits that can help even a beginner work with a new code. You can work on a ton of different codes without them taking as much time as before, and you can rely on the Windows and Microsoft products that you are used to and know work great. Now that we know a bit more about PowerShell and the benefits of using this kind of program let's start learning how to use it!

Chapter 2

Getting Those Commands Started

If you have decided to work with the PowerShell program, it is important for you to take some time to learn how to work with the variety of commands that come with it. These commands are going to be important in any kind of coding language because they are responsible for telling the computer how it needs to behave. Without these commands, or with the wrong command, the program is not going to know what actions it should take at this time. The best thing about PowerShell though is that it is simple to work with the commands that come with it, and it won't take you too long to catch on to it.

The first thing to look at is known as the naming convention. This is going to be that we want to write out the codes in the verb to noun form. This is going to ensure that things are as consistent as possible, and it is going to make it easier to learn the coding faster when we try to make longer commands. The verb is going to be the part of the command that talks about the action, and then the noun is going to be there to tell the computer where you would like the previous action to be done.

To make the command run in the proper manner on your system, you have to bring out the command prompt, which is similar to what is found in other operating systems and with other coding languages that you may try. Then, when the command prompt is up and running you would need to type in the syntax of the verb to noun and then press enter. If you wrote out the codes in the proper manner, then the process worked, and the outcome is going to be the command that you wanted.

There are going to be times when you are trying to do some code writing, and you forget how to write out the command that you would like to use. This can happen as you learn how to work with this kind of coding language. If you are uncertain about the command though, PowerShell is going to have you covered. You can just use the command of "Get" and then the program will provide you with a full list of the commands that you are able to use in PowerShell. This is like a cheat sheet that is always available and will make life easier as you get more into the coding that you would like to have happened.

Now let's, say that you use that command and you still feel lost. Or you want to have a better idea of what the different commands are able to do as you first learn how to work with this kind of system. This is easy to do as well. You just need to use the command of getting Help, and then the program can tell you more of this information.

Working with the Help Command

As you are going through PowerShell and some of the neat things that it is able to do, you will notice that it is possible to use the help files in order to give you some guidance as you go through it all. It is easy to access these help files with that Get-Help command that we talked about before. When your system has been able to read that command, it is going to bring up all of the commands that PowerShell is able to work with, along with the description of what each one does. This is useful information as a beginner because it ensures that you know what you are doing along the way.

Notice that when you are working on this kind of command, the verb and the noun are going to end up with a hyphen that helps to separate them out, and will tell the command prompt exactly what you would like to see happen there it is important that you set up the command in this manner to get it to work the way that you want.

Now, let's take this a bit further and look at how you are able to get all of this to work with some of the common administrator tasks that can show up. We are going to start out with some commands that would help you out with the text files that are available on your system. First, if there is already a file found on the system that you think you would like to read through, and then the command that is needed here would be "Get-Content." If this is the only file that you have on the system right now, it is going to show up after you place that command in your command prompt.

Of course, it is likely that you are working on a system that has more than one text file. And if you try to use the command that you have from above, the computer is going to have no idea what you would like it to pull up and bring to you. The good news here is that you can fix this problem just by adding in a few more details to ensure that it works. Make sure that you know the name of the chosen file you want to work with and then type in the command "Get-Help name Get-Content." Add in the name of the file where it says "name" on the code. This code is going to provide you with the command description as well as the information of the syntax.

Keep in mind with this one that the part of the command that says "Get-Content is going to also be able to return the contents of an item, or even return any type of file on the system to the right place. Just make sure that you are picking out the right name of the file so that the system knows what to pull up.

As you go through this, you will find that it is pretty easy to go through this and change up the syntax to make sure that you can view any of the files on your system. You can have it bring up the text on a chosen document that you want to look through, and you can have it bring up files even if they are on another system, and so much more. This is going to provide the programmer with some freedom on what they would like to do with the commands on PowerShell and can get the work done in no time.

And that is as simple and as complicated as the process needs to be! Writing codes in PowerShell is meant to be easy, and if you were worried about learning how to write a code in the past because you thought it would be too hard, let this help to put some of those fears away. Out of most of the coding languages out there, the codes that you will learn how to write in this guidebook and the ones that go along with PowerShell are going to be simple and straight to the point, and we have already spent some time looking at how you can get started using and writing some of your own!

Chapter 3

The Pipelines and Outputs in PowerShell and How These Work in Your Coding

Now that we have had some time to look at the different commands that come with PowerShell, it is time for us to look at a few of the other parts that come with this program, and how we are able to use this for our own benefits. Since the commands are not always going to be enough to provide you with the right kind of power to finish things, PowerShell has a part that is called the pipeline to make this a bit easier. You will find that these pipelines are going to be more useful in this kind of coding because they will link together the different commands that you do so that they can be stronger and handle bigger and more complex tasks than they can do all on their own.

There are so many things that these pipelines are going to be able to help you out with when you start writing some of your own codes. Because they are so important in PowerShell and they can provide you with a lot of extra power, we are going to spend some time talking about these and exploring more of what they are able to do in our codes.

Working with the Pipelines

As we have already taken some time to explore, PowerShell is going to be a program from Windows that is based on some commands. These commands are set up in order to be passed on to objects with one command and then moved over to the next object in the same manner. Each of the commands that you are working with is going to create an object, and then it will take that object and send it down the line, allowing the next command time to pick up that object.

When the object gets there, the next command is going to pick it up and will utilize the object as the input so that it is then able to take that information and use it to create some output. From here, it will take that and move it on to a third command. This keeps going until the process is all done, and it reaches the conclusion that it is supposed to. Sometimes the command chain is going to be longer, and then there are times when it is shorter. Either way, this is going to create its own pipeline, or we are able to denote this in our code with the (|) symbol.

When you are in a regular kind of command shell, the results that you get out of the pipeline are going to return to you at the same time. This means that the final result that comes with this pipeline is going to be shown in just one result, rather than you getting to see all of the individual steps that show up in the pipeline. But things are a bit different when you are working with PowerShell. When in this language, you will see the results show up through the pipeline and when just one command ends up with the result that it can show you, and then you can access it right away.

The best way to understand how this is supposed to work is by looking at an example. If you are working with the command "Get-Service" as we talked about before, you will end up getting a big rundown of each service that is already found in that framework. When all of this has completed, you will be able to see the command is giving you the display, the status of that system, and the admin name as well.

To help us see how this works a bit more, instead of just being able to see the whole of the rundown of the service on your computer, you are also going to be able to get a return from this of the services that are currently running and even working on the system. To make this action happen, you would use two commands, the "Get-Service" from before and the "Where-Object." The code that you could write out in PowerShell in order to make this happen would include:

Get-Service | Where-Object {$_status-eq 'runnin'}

As you may have seen with the code above, the pipeline operation is going to be in place, and we can use it in order to show how the two commands can be connected back with each other. The first part of the code, the Get-Service, is going to produce for us an object that will contain all of the information, in a list form that would be considered service-related. When you are using this kind of symbol, the object is going to be able to send itself over, so it ends up in the command for Where-Object. This command is going to benefit you because it is going to filter out the information based on what conditions you put into those brackets this helps to limit some of the information that you receive, so you don't end up with information overload.

Now, as we are going through this kind of process, if you find that the information is inside the brackets, you need to pay attention to whether it is right and seen as correct. If it is, then this object will be able to make its way through the pipeline that you made. But if it seems that there is information that is false, this information won't make the cut and will not filter out. This means to make sure that in the end, you only have the information that you want, and nothing else.

With the previous example, we also added on a part for -eq. This is important because it means that the property of the status needs to be equal to the string that you are running. It is important that you are able to glance and look at all of the properties that you have used inside the file where Status is a part that will generate an object with the help of your command. When you do have one or more object go through the pipeline, then you will be able to access the properties similar to the process that we used with the command Where-Object.

At this point, it is time to move on and look a bit at what we would want to do if we needed to get some limitations on the information that we were getting. Sometimes, it is possible that a lot of information will flood you and this can make it difficult when you just want to get some specific information, and you don't want to look through all of the information that is there.

This is not a big problem in PowerShell because there are a few steps that you can take to extend out the pipeline so that it will provide you with the right information, without you have to sort through everything all of the time. The best syntax that you can use to make sure that you can place the right restrictions on your code includes:

Get-Service |
where {$_.statust -eq 'running'} |
select displayname

With this example, we are going to see that the command for Select-Object is going to be the first to receive the object that you are working with. This illustration is going to show us the where alias that you need to use as well, which means that it is not necessary to work and list out the Where-Object all of the time. Then we will find that this is going to happen again when we work with the alias for select as well. This is going to help out because it makes the PowerShell code easier to write out and a bit shorter.

When you decide to work with more than one pipeline or three at this time, you need to remember that we are doing a process of operating with the objects. This means that all of the commands that you try to add into the syntax will be able to create some of their own objects, which will be received by the next command that you are working on. And then the final command that you wrote out is going to be responsible for generating out the object that you want. This is going to output the results that you are looking for the entire time.

As you can see, there is a lot that you are able to work with when it comes to the pipelines that show up in your code. These are going to help you to search for the things that you want on the computer, put in the limitations that you want, and so much more. Learning how to use these, and practicing with some of the codes that we have provided in this chapter can make it easier to see how PowerShell is meant to work.

Chapter 4

The Different Operators in This Coding Language

In the last chapter, we spent some of our time exploring the pipelines that are used in PowerShell and how you will be able to add these to your code in order to make sure you streamline the work that you do in this kind of coding language. These pipelines are going to make it easier to sort out any kind of information that you have on the system and will make it so much easier to change up some of the files that you would like to pull up and use. Basically, these pipelines are going to allow you to take a string of commands that you have and connect them together, allowing for some filtering out of the objects that you want, and then the information that is the output or the results will show up on your screen.

If you have ever had a chance to do some coding in the past, even with a different language, you will notice that they are going to hold onto a few different operations. These are going to be valuable in coding because they can be used by the programmer in order to create a few expressions in the code. This is something that does still happen in the PowerShell language; they are just going to show up in a different manner than we saw with some of the other common programming languages.

This is why we need to spend some time looking at the variety of operators that are already available in the PowerShell system, ones that you are able to use, and even some of the codes we have explored in this guidebook are going to have these written inside as well. With this in mind, let's explore some of the different types of operators and wildcards that are available to use and make coding easier in PowerShell.

Comparison Operators

They are a lot of different operators that you are able to explore when you are working on some code. And the first ones that we are going to spend time exploring are the comparison operators. These are going to be used in your code in order to compare different values. Any time that you have a few items that are placed in the code and you want to compare the different values, and then you would use the comparison operators. Some of the options that you are going to be able to use when it comes to the comparison operators used in PowerShell will include:

1. **Eq:** This is going to be for equal to.

2. **-ne:** this one means not equal to.

3. **-gt:** This one means greater than.

4. **-get:** This one means that it is greater than or equal to.

5. **-lt:** This one stands for less than.

6. **-le:** This one stands for equal to or less than.

7. **-like:** This one is going to use one of the wildcards that we will talk about later in order to find a pattern that is matching.

8. **-notlike:** This one is going to bring out the wildcards again in order to find some of the patterns that are not matching.

9. **-match:** This is going to rely on some of the regular expressions to help us find the patterns that match.

10. **-notmatch:** These are going to work with the regular expressions from before to help find the nonmatching patterns

11. **-contains:** This is going to determine for us whether the value we have on the left side of the operator is going to be the same value as the value we have on the right side.

12. **-notcontains**: This one is going to determine whether the value that we have on the left of our operator doesn't have the same value as what we are going to find on the right side of the operator.

13. **-replace:** This is the one that will be able to replace part or all of the value that we can see on the left side of our operators.

It is easy to work in PowerShell with these operators because they make sure that we can compare all of the parts of the code that we need. You will need to do some studying and then figure out which one is going to work the best for your needs. All of them are useful, but it often depends on what you want to have done in your code.

Looking at the Wildcards

We need to take a quick break from the discussion on operators and explore a bit about a topic of wildcards and how they work in PowerShell. With the wildcards, you are using them to try to do a search for an item which you know is found in one of your files, but you are not able to remember what the name of that file is in the first place. We are able to still look for it, but we need to be able to create a new expression that can help us to express that can compare the values at the same time

What our options are in this kind of situation is to not just guess and get things lost in the computer, but we can use a wildcard as one of our operators, or even as the compared value to help us find the things that we want. There are a few different types of wildcards that we are able to work with, and that can work the best with PowerShell, and these include:

1. **(*):** This is going to match zero or more of any character that you would like:

2. **(?):** This one is going to help out because it is able to match any one character that you choose and add with it

3. **[char-char]:** This one is going to help us to match a range of characters that are all in a line together.

4. **[char..]:** This one is going to be used because it is going to match any one character that is found inside a set of other characters that you defined.

You may think that, when we look at the wildcards, they are going to look similar to the comparison operators of -like and -not like that we were talking about above. These are similar, and you get the benefit of being able to use these to find the files that you want, even when you are not sure what the name of the file is, or you are unsure about which of the files you would like to be able to use. Let's take a look at the code syntax that is below to get a better understanding of how this is going to work and how it is going to work:

et-process |
*where {$_.company -like "*google*"}*

In the code that we are working with above, the asterisk is going to be our wildcard, and it is going to be used to help us match zero, and often more, characters. This is going to be useful because it ensures that you get some results, even if you are not able to pick out the exact name of the file that you want to work with. This is true whether or not the folder has been stored under the same variation that you have now or a different one.

PowerShell can also step it up by completing what is known as regular expressions inside of your code. These are going to be based on the classes of regular expressions that you can find when you use the Microsoft framework that is .NET

Adding in Some of the Logical Operators

Now we need to move on to some of the other operators that you are able to work with, known as the logical operators. These operators are going to help you work with some of the expressions that are going to come with two or more conditions attached to them. This is going to be done whenever you would like to work with more than one comparison, and it is needed to tell your program to take action or just stay where it is

This may sound more complicated, and you may be worried about how you are going to work with these logical operators, but to make sure that you are able to work with them in just one expression, you just need to take one of the logical operators that we are going to talk about below ad then make sure that it is linked in the correct manner to a condition. These types of operators are going to be used in order to specify what logic you would like to implement an evaluation that looks at more than one condition at a time.

With this mind, it is important to note that there is more than one type of logical operators that are available for you to work with. Some of these are going to include:

1. **-and:** This is going to be used when both conditions have to be true before we are able to evaluate our expression as true.

2. **-or:** This is where you would need just one, but sometimes both conditions to be true before you can evaluate the expression as something that is true.

3. **-not:** This one is going to be when the condition has to be false before you can go through and evaluate the expression as something that is true:

4. **(!):** This is going to be the operator that is used when we need both of the conditions in the statement to be false before we can evaluate the expression as true.

The Arithmetic Operators

PowerShell is also going to have some room to handle arithmetic operators. These are going to look pretty familiar to you because if you have ever attended a math class, then a lot of these are going to show up. With this kind of language, you can work with these operations in order to make sure that different parts of the code are added together, taken apart, and more. You just need to make sure you are using the right kind of operator I the process. A few of the most common operators that you can use that fit in this category with PowerShell are going to include:

1. **(+):** This one is going to add two values, or two parts of the code together.

2. **(-):** This one is going to subtract two values, or parts of the code, from one another.

3. **(~):** This one is going to take one value and will turn it over into a negative number:

4. **(*):** This one is going to take two values that you have and multiply them together.

5. **(/):** This one is going to divide the two values of your choice.

6. **(%):** This one is going to return the remainder of the numbers that you tried to divide from each other.

As you can see, most of the arithmetic operators that you will use are going to be easy to work with and will not take that much to learn and remember. And they are going to show up on a pretty regular basis when you are doing some coding in PowerShell. You can use them to do a lot of different things, and it is important to review them and keep them on hand so you can use them when you would like.

We just spent some time talking about the different operators that you are able to use in your own coding. Adding in some operators is pretty simple to do, and this can add in a lot of the functionality that you need with any code that you would like to write out in PowerShell. They can help you to compare different parts of the code, they can help you to look up the files and information that you need on the system, and so much more.

Chapter 5

The Drives and the Providers

A s you go through and prepare some of the codes and the work that you need for PowerShell, there are going to be a variety of folders and files that you are able to choose from. But before you do any of that, you have to double check that you are giving the system the right name for the path. The pathname is going to be pretty simple with Windows because you are just going to work with the C:\ and then add in the name that you want with the file or the folder. Any time that you want to go through and find a file system that is specific, you need to double check that PowerShell has the right name for that drive, so it is actually able to find the information.

Another part that a lot of programmers like when they work on PowerShell is that there are a few drives that may not already be on your system, but can be supported with the PowerShell program. This makes it easier to have information and extra storage for some of the tasks that you would like to finish. A good example of what we mean by this is the scaler drive. This drive is going to help you out because you can work with the built-in scalers that also behave well with PowerShell. Let's take a closer look at some of these drives and the different providers that you can use with PowerShell to get a better idea of what they are all about.

The Providers for PowerShell

The first thing that we need to look at in this chapter is that with PowerShell, we are going to work with a core. We can find this core inside the data store of our provider for PowerShell. There are a few different providers that can work with this kind of language, but one of the best, since it comes from the same company as PowerShell, is Microsoft .NET. this one is able to show you what you need to connect the data stores through the service.

Many of the providers that you are going to need at this point are pre-built into the program. If you want to look at the full list of the providers that are available with PowerShell, you would just need to write out the command of "Get-PSProvider | select Name." but there are a few ones that we need to take a moment to talk about now, and they will include:

1. **Alias:** There are going to be some aliases that you can create and use in order to call up a lot of the popular commands that you want to use in this language, without having to write them all out.

2. **Certificate:** This is going to be a process that you can do through Windows that helps with certificates of digital signatures.

3. **Environment:** This is going to be a scaler that works with the Windows environment.

4. **FIleSystem:** this is going to be the Windows file system drives, folders, and files.

5. **Function:** These are going to include all of the different functions that work in PowerShell.

6. **Registry:** This is going to be the registry that is available through the Windows programs.

7. **Scaler:** These are going to be the scalers that come with PowerShell and that we talked about just a moment ago.

As we take a look at what this list is all going to entail, it is easy to notice that a lot of the processes and providers that we are talking about will be a part of Windows. And this is because PowerShell and Windows are going to work well together as PowerShell is a product of Windows. There are non-Windows options that you can do with PowerShell, but often the Windows option is going to be one of the best for you to use.

What Are Some of the Drives Built into This Program

Now that we know a bit about some of the best providers that work with PowerShell, it is time to take this a bit further and look at the drives, and which ones are already found automatically inside the system of PowerShell. These drives are going to be ones that you will use on a regular basis in order to make sure that you can return data from the providers that are listed above in an easy and efficient manner.

Basically, the data for the file system is going to be exposed over to the drive-in PowerShell that will correspond to that drive in Windows. The C drive is then going to be able to access all of the data by a file system which is then going to expose the Windows C drive back to the system. This can sound confusing, but the simple code that you are going to use to make all of this happen will include the following:

Get-PSDrive | sort Provider, Name

With the code above, you are able to sort out the information starting with the provider, and then you will get the name. this is useful because it allows the sorting to be easier because all of your providers come out grouped together. Then you can go through each of the providers and see how many drives are there for the provider to hold. You will also be able to look through the code we have above and see the root information that is necessary to make sure you can locate the store of the target data that you wish to display.

Creating Your Own Drive

Another cool thing that you are able to do when you want to work with the PowerShell program, even as a beginner, is that you can use a variety of codes in order to create one of your own drives. While the PowerShell program is going to provide you with a ton of drives that are already on the system and ready to use, there are times when these will not be enough, and the drives are not going to provide you with the information or the actions that are just right for what you want to do. This is when you will want to go through the process of creating a new drive on your system and changing it around, so it meets all of your needs.

These new drives are going to have to have some basis, even just a tiny bit, on some of the providers that are found on the PowerShell system already. This may seem like a pain, but it actually makes the work a bit easier to handle. But, you are able to use this information to make something that is brand new and easier to work with.

So, with that in mind, it is time to start creating our own new drive for PowerShell. First, you need to work with the New-PSDrive command like we had brought up before. Let's look at the syntax that we would be able to use in order to create our own drive to see how easy it is. we are going to make a drive that is known as ps.

New-PSDrive -Name ps
-PSProvider FileSystem -Root $pshome

As you take a look at the code that is above, you will notice that it is pretty simple to work with. You are able to work with a code that is as simple as what we just did and create a whole new drive that works in the PowerShell system. You knew that this system was supposed to be easy to learn and work with, but you probably never imagined that it would be that easy to work on the various tasks that come with it.

With the illustration that we just did above, you may notice that it is going to take a bit of time to identify which name you would like to call up the new drive, and it is going to keep on so that you can name the root and the provider at the same time. When it is time to go through the process of running this illustration, PowerShell knows that it needs to make up a new drive at the same time. PowerShell, when it is done with the work it is doing, is going to display the information that is needed, so that you are able to look and see what is present on that drive.

When you get to this point, you may notice that any information that is being shown to you is not going to show the traditional name that you are used to, but it is going to show off the root name instead. After you have been able to write out the new drive and you are done creating it, you can use it in the exact same manner as you would with any of the other drives that are already built-into the system for you. You just need to change up the location for operating that new drive so that it is going to work the way that you would like. The syntax that you need to use to make this happen includes:

cd ps: \

Then, depending on how you want to write out the code that you have, there could be times when you would like to either delete or remove a drive that you had spent time defining or creating, and this is simple to do as well. You just need to work with the command for Remove-PSDrive. It is important to keep track of the drives that you are in because you are not able to delete out one of the drives that you are in the process of working on. If you try to do this, an error is going to show up, so keep this in mind as you do your work.

As you are working with the drives, whether you handle some that are already automatically in the system or you create one of your own, you have to remember that the new ones are only going to be considered valid during the session that you created it in. this is going to be helpful because you won't have to go through all of it after you are done with the program, and you will not need to remove or delete any of the processors or the drive unless you have another reason to do this.

The reason that you don't need to do all of this work or even worry about it is that the program is going to be able to automatically do this when you close out of the program. It is sometimes a hassle to have this happen when you are in the process of doing a few different systems, and they all need the same new drives, but since it is only about a line or two of code to make this new drive, it often doesn't take that long to fix the problem.

Creating a new drive in PowerShell is a fun experience and can help you to learn how to work on some more of the coding that you would like to get done for yourself. You get the choice of creating your own, or even using a drive that is automatically going to come with the program, it all depends on what you are trying to do with the code and which option out of the two seems to work the best for you.

When you are ready to create one of your own new drives, don't be scared that it is going to be too hard to do or that you are not going to be able to handle all of the steps that need to be done. We just spent a few minutes learning how this works, and finding out that it is easier than you would think. Just use some of the steps above to help you create one of these new drives so that you can do some practicing and get the hang of it so you can use that information to make it work for your own coding needs.

Chapter 6

More Work with PowerShell –
How to Work with the Quotes and Strings in
PowerShell

There are a few different types of syntaxes that you are able to choose to work with when PowerShell is your chosen language for writing out codes. The majority of them are going to be called string values. What this means is that they are going to be an argument that is passed over the commands. You will also see that the strings are going to be enclosed with the help of a single quote, but you do have the option of using the double quote if you would like. In this chapter, it is important that we take some time to look at what these strings are and how they work inside your codes so that you can use them to write out some of the codes that you need later on.

What Are the String Values

The first thing that we need to take a look at here is what the string values are all about When you get started with writing out some codes, if you see that there is some kind of text within that code that has a quote around it no matter where it is, then this is going to be your string value. Knowing this, as long as the text doesn't use scalers or have any special characters, you are going to be able to make the decision on your own about whether you would like to use single or double-quotes. Special characters can also come in with some special rules that we need to follow, but we will look into those a bit more closely later on.

Any time that you are writing out a new code that is going to work with some regular strings remember that the double and the single quotes are going to end up with the same meaning within your code. The important part is that when you do this, whether you use the double quotes or the single quotes, your text should not end up holding onto special characters.

It is also going to matter whether you stop and start the quotes in the same manner. You will get an error message if you start out a new string using single quotes and then end it with a double quote. The compiler is going to view both of these in a different manner, so it is best to choose which one is going to be your choice, and then stick with that.

There is also the possibility of wanting to use a quote inside of the string that you are creating. This is possible, but the rules for doing it are going to be different than what you may have seen before. The quote that is inside of the string needs to be different than what you use for the string itself to avoid confusion. A good example of how you could write out the quote inside the string if you choose to do this includes:

Write-Output "String 'in' quotes"

Write-Output 'String "in" quotes'

If you do mess up with this one and you have a double quote that is inside the double quote that you are using for your string, or a single quote within the single quote, the code is not going to be read out in the manner that you would like. Any time that you are trying to add in some quotes to a code that you are writing, make sure that you pay attention to how you are writing these quotes to see that they are done in the right manner, or there are issues with the code and the answers that you get will not be what you are looking for.

Adding in Special Characters

We already spent a bit of time talking about the special characters and how these were going to work a bit differently when you wanted to handle the string values and the quotes from before. But now we need to spend some time looking at these special characters and how they are going to work with our needs.

In the section above, along with some of the examples that we provided, you were able to choose the type of quote that you would most like to use. In these examples, it is possible to work with either the single or the double quote because they are going to mean the same thing when it is all done. It is only important that the same quote is used as the front and the back of the string or you are going to end up with an error in your code.

39

However, there are going to be times when the choice in quote type is going to matter, and there will be some kind of distinction that shows up between the single and double quote. The single quote is going to be the part that is responsible for the literal handling of the string, and then the double quote is going to help you to escape any of those special characters that may show up in the code.

When we have a special character, and we precede it with the (`) or the backtick, it is going to take on a specific action that you wouldn't be able to accomplish at all if these kinds of symbols were not in place. Some of the characters that are considered as special in PowerShell and that you may need at some point when you are working on the PowerShell program includes:

1. `o: This is going to insert in a null value for us.

2. `a. This is going to send us an alert, which is sometimes going to be a bell and other times a beep to the speakers on your computer system

3. `b. This is going to insert a backspace into your work:

4. `": This one is going to make sure that a double quote is inserted into the mix.

5. `'. This is going to insert a single quote into the mix.

6. `v. This one will make sure that a vertical is inserted in the right place.

7. `**`t.**` This one is going to make sure that a horizontal tab is inserted.

8. `**`r.**` This one is going to make sure that a carriage return is inserted.

9. `**`n.**` This one is going to help us insert a new line for the programmer when they want to use that space for text.

10. `**`f.**` This one is going to make sure that the form feed is inserted.

One of the methods that you can use in order to really understand how the concepts above are going to work is to do some of the coding and put them to work. Bring out your command line and type in the following code, with some of the different parts present that you need, to see what comes up for you with the special characters above:

Write-Output (""`n `tText includes: + ""`n `t" escaped `' characters, 1n")

The first character that we are going to see that is able to escape out of this illustration is going to be the 'n. Then the next one will be our I which will end up with the ab being inserted into the code writing that you do. Make sure that you take notice of the backtick that we were able to use in the first line, but see that it is not going to be considered one of the escape character. However, it is going to be used to show that the illustration present is going to continue on.

From here we added in the double quotes and these will then show up around the escaped character, and they will then have a backtick ahead of them so that you are going to be able to get those quotes to show up when you ask for the output as well. If you spend your time trying to get the characters to escape even though they were within the string that was enclosed with just the single quote, then the special characters and the backticks are not going to show up with this kind of output. This is due to the fact that when you use single quotes it is going to handle all of the information that you have in a more literal manner

System_String object members

Any time that you are trying to do some of the strings in PowerShell, you want to make sure that you always handle them in the same manner that you would if they were System_String objects. This is a good thing to always remember because it can benefit your code writing with a lot of properties and extra methods along the way.

As we talked about a bit earlier, the "Get-Member command is going to be used here to help you retrieve the members of an object as they are being pushed through any pipeline that you create. Since the string is also going to be passed just with what happened to the objects you are going to be able to use the same command on one of these strings. A good code that lets us see how this is going to work will be below:

 "test output" | Get-Member

When you take the time to type this out and execute it, you will see that the string we are working on here is going to have the ability to support a few methods or more. These methods may include some different options like a 'Substring' or "GetType based on what you would like to do with the code. You can also go through and scroll through some of the information that you have a bit to figure out the length property, which is a good way to figure out how much information or how many characters are found in that string right now.

We need to stop here and take a look at some of the code that is going to help us see how this works. For this example, we are going to say that we want to look at the method of Substring and we want to be able to use the command of Get-Member in order to make sure that we get ahold of the information. A good syntax of the code that you can use to make this happen will be below:

"test output" |
Get-Member Substring |
Format-List

After you have had a chance to go through and then run this code, you will find that there are going to be a few details that are present which are meant to tell us the proper manner to utilize this method. There are also going to be two styles of approach that you are able to use when it comes to working on this method. They are going to include:

System.String Substring(Int32 startIndex)
System.String Substring(Int32 start Index Int32 length)

With the first option that we have above, you are providing the target string to the system as well as the integer that it needs to use. This kind of integer is going to be used in order to specify the position from where you would like to see the starting position of your substring. When it is in place properly, it is going to make it so that the substring will return to the right position and then continue on this path until it has been able to reach the strings' end. This process is going to make things easier if you are planning on looking at the whole string, but you would like to make sure that you start out this process in a specific location of your choice.

The first option is often a good one for the programmer to choose because it is going to make it possible to have the test output show up, and then it is going to start with the position that you choose for the substring. Remember you are free to choose any number that you want to place here as long as it is already found in the code.

Then there is the second example as well, and there are times when you would want to work with this part too depending on how your coding works. With the second option, you are going to need to provide the target string as well as the starting point and length of the substring you are using. If you want to make sure that your program starts itself off at a specific spot on your string, and you only want to let it so that the program reads through a few lines of it all, then working on that second method listed above is going to be the best.

As you can see, there can be a lot of potential power that comes with the PowerShell system. And you are able to use some of the information that we just went through, and some of the codes in this chapter, to help you prepare and really learn how to work with strings, making codes easier to write in the PowerShell language.

Chapter 7

How to Execute Your Commands

You will find that when you work with the PowerShell program, it isn't just going to be about scripting, it is also going to spend some time working on how you can run the commands. Scripting entails entering the keywords into the text editor you have, saving the script, and then doing some tests by running that script. Executing the commands is going to be more active. This is because the commands are going to be entered into the shell, and then the administrators are able to go through and modify those commands to get the effect that they want before executing.

In the process, PowerShell is going to run those commands to immediate impact. Continually using PowerShell is going to teach users to learn to take those same commands and then enter them into a text editor and then save them using the file extension of .ps1. when this is all done, you have a script that works in PowerShell. Whatever commands are run often enough to copy into a script are the ones that can be automated, saving you a lot of time typing and running the command like with traditional coding.

To start with, though, we need to be able to do an investigation of the structure of the command. There are going to be some important formatting tips to keep in mind when you are working with the command. First, do not allow any spaces to show up between the text and the dash that you want to work with, the parameters that you are setting are always going, to begin with a dash, and make sure that there is some kind of space that shows up between the parameters, especially if you have more than one. These are going to help us to make sure that any kind of cmdlets that we make in PowerShell will work the way that we want.

These may seem pretty simple, but if you mess up on some of these in the beginning when you are writing out your code, then your foundation is not going to work well when you start to increase the complexity in the code. Having these down will make your work shorter and faster, as soon as you learn how to navigate them away as well.

There are also going to be a ton of different ways that you are able to expand out with the cmdlets, but there are two that most programmers of PowerShell are going to focus on including the truncation and the alias. We talked about the alias a bit before and how it is going to be a shortened version of your code. This can be done with any of the coding that you do on a regular basis. This helps to shorten up the work that you need to do and can make a big difference in how easy writing codes can be in the process.

Another thing to take a look at here is the help command. This is going to be the most effective method that you can use when it is time to expand out some of the usable knowledge that is found in PowerShell. Mastering this language in order to use it from day one effectively is really not required because you are able to use the parameters that you want and some aliases in order to help with the functions.

The next level of self-learning that we need to know for this one is the Show-Command because it is going to attempt to handle all of the parameters that are there for any kind of command and will go through and complete the syntax for you. What another coding language is out there that you can use that will help to complete the codes that you need, will give you some help with the meanings and the uses of the different codes that you have, and will make coding as easy as possible in the process.

One thing that is important when working on any of the commands that come with PowerShell is that if you are not going to read through the help files that come with it, then you aren't going to find yourself effective in this kind of coding language. In fact, you may as well give up now if you are not willing to get through the help system and learn how to work with it, then you will not be able to learn how to administer some of the products like Windows with it, and you should just stick with GUI.

Using the help system that PowerShell is able to provide is going to be critical when it comes to expanding out the usable knowledge of the inner working of PowerShell. The developers who created this help section had the expectation that it was going to be a big resource of knowledge for any user who wanted to learn how to work with PowerShell. It is there to locate some of the commands that you do not know so that you can perform a given operation that you want. And even when you get an error message to show up, you can use the help section to make sure that you are doing the command in the proper manner, and that you have used the right syntax along the way.

Creating commands is going to work a bit differently in the PowerShell environment than you would see with some of the other coding languages that are out there. Learning how to make this work and the steps that you need to take to write out commands in PowerShell, and how to use the help function to make sure you know the commands that you need, can make all the difference.

Chapter 8

How Can I Format My Data and Handle Objects, Tables, Properties, and Methods

The use of objects in PowerShell can sometimes turn into a very confusing element of working in this language, but at the same time, it is going to be one of the most important concepts that come with this language because it is able to affect all of the things that happen inside the shell. But first, we need to take a look at what an object actually is.

In PowerShell, when we talk about an object, we are going to see that it is a row in the table. It is going to represent just one single thing, including a service or an individual process. PowerShell is going to be limited in how much information it is able to display at one time about any of the given objects that it has. The shell is going to be able to create a table in memory of the complete details of a function, but it is only going to present what the screen has enough room in order to display.

For the most part, in order to see all of the information that is available for a command, a piped cmdlet to your output file is going to be necessary. It is possible to change up the default display to show information other than what the PowerShell decides is relevant, but in most cases, it is going to be easier for you to create a not output file to find all of the data that is appropriate. A good example of the syntax that you can write out in PowerShell in order to make one of these output files for a system process would look like the following:

Get-Process | ConvertTo-HTML | Out-File processes.html

One thing that we need to consider here though is that the cmdlet is not going to filter out the columns. Instead, it is going to be able to create a file that is HTML to contain all of these things. In addition to the information being displayed in columns, each table row is going to have actions that are associated with it. Those actions are going to include what actions you would like the operating system to take with all of the listed processes that are in the table row.

You will find that the operating system can do a lot of things with the process that you are in including close that process, kill it, refresh the data that is in it, or wait for the process to be able to exit on its own, just to name a few different possibilities. Any time that you have a command that is going to produce an output and it is the one that is running, then the output is going to become a table inside of the memory. The piping output from one command over to another is going to cause the whole of the table to make its way through your created pipeline at this point.

With this process, the table is not going to be filtered down to be a smaller number of columns until every command has run and

PowerShell needs to display some form of output on the screen. But this brings up the question as to why PowerShell is going to be so focused on manipulating these objects in the first place? This is going to be revealed when we take a look at some of the ideology that is behind the development of PowerShell.

To start with this one, Windows is going to be considered an operating system that is object-oriented in nature. The software that is able to run with Windows has to also be object-oriented, so choosing to structure data as a set of objects is going to be easy since this is the way that the operating system is set up to handle things.

Objects are also going to make things a bit easier on the administrator, and they can provide more of the flexibility and power that are needed. Other programs that have a shell that does not have this orientation to being objected focused are going to parse the text in order to help the shell present in order to recognize the desired patterns that are in the text, instead of doing a direct object manipulation.

And this is why PowerShell is going to work so well with Windows. The engine that is behind it is going to be designed in order to recognize any calls for specific objects, so you will not have to go through and learn the process to parsing text for recognizable strings of data. This doesn't mean that you will not have to do some kind of manipulation of the data at some point, but it is going to cut down on how much of this you have to do in order to see success with the coding. Arguments that come with the best methodology to use are not going to be the end goal because you are simply focusing on the communication that happens natively with the various technologies of Windows.

Now through this guidebook, we took some time to expose some of the inner workings of PowerShell, and we say that some of the data tables for these objects that have been stored in the memory are not going to display the complete table when you are done with the execution of cmdlet. How then are we to access the complete information, assuming that a given output is not going to display pieces of information that are pertinent to the task or the function that we are trying to work on?

In logical terms, the help system is one of the first places to look, but we know that this particular system is only going to contain data on cmdlets, the syntax that comes with them, and some of the background information in the form of articles "about' the topic. Therefore, the answer to this question is going to lie in the cmdlet Get-Member.

Now that we have some of this information ready to go, it is time to actually look at some of the scripting's that come with working on Windows PowerShell and some of the important things that you are able to do with this to make the tables and more work in this language.

While you may not think too much about how some of the text is going to be displayed in the console of PowerShell, there is quite a bit that is going on behind the scenes when you are working with this language. Think about all of the different kinds of commands that you could run on the PowerShell, with each of these having thousands of different values and names for the objects. PowerShell isn't able to just return all of the raw output that comes with this because it would end up being a mess.

The good news is that PowerShell is going to do a great job of automatically formatting the output that we are able to get. However, with this in mind, there may be some times when we want our own method of formatting, one that is not going to work the same as the automatic function of PowerShell. One command that allows you to change up the format that is the default is the Format-Table cmdlet.

To understand how this kind of cmdlet is going to work, we first need to have some time to understand the formatting type that comes with PowerShell and the system that it has. To demonstrate this, we need to call the Get-Process cmdlet.

S C:\> Get-Process | ft

Handles	NPM(K)	PM(K)	WS(K)	CPU(s)	Id	SI	ProcessName
87	5	1108	4728	0.00	1432	13	CExecSvc
39	4	1680	3024	0.00	10820	13	cmd
94	8	3696	7716	0.09	11108	13	conhost
224	11	1872	4688	0.19	908	13	csrss
0	0	0	4	0	0		Idle
810	24	5124	15120	0.17	7824	13	lsass

The thing that we need to remember here is that the Format-Table function is going to force our text so that it is going to be displayed in a table, but the output of Get-Process is already going to be in the tabular format. We could choose to do a pipe of the Get-Process directly to the Format-Table functions, but it would have no difference in the look of the output that we are working with.

However, what is going to happen if we work with the function of Select-Object to help us handle all of the properties that get returns of Get-Process? By default, we have to know that the Get-Process function is only going to show us a few of the properties that are going to be important. You can see that the output would end up with the format of a list because it is not going to be able to fit in all of the properties in the screen.

However, we know that it is possible to get the screen to fit with all of the properties that we want. We just need to go through and change up the formatting default in the process of overriding. This is where the Format-Table is going to come into play. By taking the output and piping it of any command, including the one that we have here, we can use the code below to make sure that the output the PowerShell program gives us shows up in a format that is tabular.

```
PS    C:\>    Get-Process    |    Select-Object    -Property
Name,Id,Description,FileVersion,Threads -First 1 | Format-Table
```

Name	Id	Description	FileVersion	Threads

CExecSvc   1432   Container   Execution   Agent   10.0.14393.0
(rs1_release.160715-1616) {8008, 8688, 6340, 5184}

The Format-Table cmdlet is going to be an option that will be the last one that is used inside of your pipeline. Like some of the other cmdlets that are used for formatting, the Format-Table is not going to return any objects to the pipeline and this should always be the last one to be used.

The Format-Table has a lot of different options that you are able to manipulate the text once it has been displayed as well. Some of the parameters that are common for this one will include AutoSize, which is going to help us to automatically size the output by basing it on your console size, and HideTableHeaders, which isn't going to display the property names of the objects for you.

As you can see, going through and being able to make some changes to the codes that you are writing and ensuring that you can get the right table to show up, and even in the right size based on the type of console, and the size of it that is available, is a fairly easy process to work on in PowerShell, just like many of the other codes that you may work on.

Chapter 9

Working with Remote in a Practical Manner

The next topics that we are going to spend some time on here are how you are able to do a few functions with the help of the PowerShell program. We are going to focus our attention on how to do the remote and then also the multitasking functions in this kind of coding language to ensure that we can see some more of the codes that we want to write and that we can use PowerShell in many different manners. Let's get started seeing how both of these functions are going to work with PowerShell.

Working with the Remote Functions

The remoting function on PowerShell will help you to run some of the commands that you have, or access the full PowerShell sessions on a system of Windows that is remote. It is going to be a similar process to the SSH for accessing the remote terminals on some of the other operating systems that are there. PowerShell is going to have the default of being locked down, so you will need to make sure that the PowerShell Remoting before you use it. This setup is going to process a bit more complex compared to using a workgroup rather than a domain, which can happen when you are doing something like a home network, but we are going to walk through the process, so we are able to do this the proper manner.

The first step that we want to do here is to get the PowerShell Remoting to work on our PC so that we are able to make the remote connections that we want. On the PC that you want to use, you have to get the PowerShell program open and make sure that you give yourself the privileges of the administrator to get it done. If you are working with the Windows 10 version of the operating system, you can press on Windows+X and then choose PowerShell (Admin) from the menu that is there.

If you are working with some of the older versions of the Windows operating system, then you just need to type in "PowerShell" and right-click on the results that are given. Make sure to click so that you are able to Run as administrator as well. IN the window that comes up for PowerShell, type in the cmdlet that is below and then press on enter:

Enable -PSRemoting -Force

This command may look simple, but it is going to make sure that the service of WinRM is able to start up, and then it will set it up to start automatically any time that you begin your system. It is also going to go through and create a firewall rule that will allow for some incoming connections. The -Force part of our code is going to be the one that tells our PowerShell to perform these actions, without you having to go through and write more code or prompting the system each time you use it.

If you have a PC that is part of a domain, then this is the final step that you need to go through. You can skip the rest of the steps and head right over to how to test the connection. However, if you are working on computers that are part of a workgroup, then there is going to be a bit more to do in order to get the process done.

One thing to note here is that your success in being able to set up this remoting is going to depend entirely on the setup of the network. Remoting could disable and sometimes enabled, automatically by a group policy that is configured by the admin. You might also not have the right permissions in place on your computer or your system in order to run PowerShell as an administrator. As always, if you are not the one who has this kind of power, then check with the actual admins of the system before you go through the process at all.

Now, if you need to continue on with the process and your PC is not part of a domain, then the next step that we need to work on is setting up the Workgroup that you wish to follow. At this point, we have already taken the time to enable Remoting on the PC that you want to connect to. Keep in mind here that if you would like this type of Remoting to work, you need to configure the network to be private, rather than having it be a public network.

The next thing that you need to do is make sure to configure the TrustedHosts setting on both the PC to which you want to connect and the PC or the multiple PCs that you would like to connect from. This ensures that computers will trust each other. There are two methods that you can use in order to get this one done.

The first option is when you are working off a home network. If this is the kind of network that you are using, and you want to make sure that you can trust any of the other PCs that would like to connect in a remote manner, then you would need to make sure that you can run the following code as the main Administrator:

Set-Item wsman:\localhost\client\trsutedhosts *

The asterisk that we added in is going to be an example that we talked about before when we were looking at different operators, and it is going to encompass all of the PCs. If you want to restrict how many computers, or which computers, are able to connect with your own, you would want to take out that asterisk and then have a comma-separated list of all the computer names or the IP addresses of the PCs that you approve for this connection.

After you have been able to run the command that is above, you can then restart the service for WinRM so that the new settings that you put on are able to take effect. And when this is done, we want to write out the code below to continue on, while hitting Enter when we are done:

Restart-Service WinRM

At this point, we are going to test the connection hat we have. now that the PC, or more than one computer, is set up for the PowerShell

Remoting, we need to do a test on the connection that we did and make sure that it is actually going to work the way that we want. Using the PC that we would like to access the remote system from, you need to make sure to use the following code. Remember here that the COMPUTER part here needs to be replaced with the IP address or the name of the PC that is remote, and then when it is done, hit the Enter button to continue:

Test-WsMan COMPUTER

This is a simple command, but it is going to be there to help us know whether or not the WinRM is running on your remote PC. If it is able to complete its work successfully, you are going to see information about the remote computer's WinRM service in the window, and this is going to signify that the program is enabled and that it is time to get the computers to communicate together. If you get an error message, you may need to double check that the program is running and working the way that you want.

And now that we know that the process is working the way that we want and we have had some time to test out what we are doing, it is time to work on executing a single remote command. To run a type of command that you would like to use on your remote system, you need to work with the cmdlet that is known as Invoke-Command, and the syntax below is going to help you to get this done:

Invoke-Command -ComputerName COMPUTER -ScriptBlock { COMMAND } -credential USERNAME

Let's take a look at this code a bit. The part that says COMPUTER is going to represent the IP address or the name of the PC that is the remote one. Then the COMMAND part is going to be the command that you want to tell the remote computer to do. And we can also look at the USERNAME part because this is going to be the username that you as the programmer, will want to run the command on your chosen remote computer. You are also going to be prompted to enter a password for the username before you are able to do all of this.

And that is all there is to it. If you followed the codes and the steps that we listed out above, and you made sure to test out the program to make sure that it works, you will be able to access a computer remotely, even giving it the commands that you want from far away.

Chapter 10

Working with Multitasking Functions in PowerShell

One of the key characteristics that come with the PowerShell program is the way that it is able to take on more than one task at a time. This is in contrast to what we see with some of the earlier versions of this language, and some of the other programming languages that are out there, but you will find that the newer versions do allow for this. This can be nice because you can do some of the jobs that take too long to load up, while still using your shell for some of the other tasks that you want to get done.

In the past, this was not possible. You had to spend time waiting for the program to finish, even if it was one that would take a few hours to finish because of its nature, and then you could use the shell or do any other kind of coding. This could be tiring and tedious and don't allow you to get much done in an efficient manner. But thanks to some of the changes that have now been implemented in PowerShell, this is no longer a problem. It allows you to do more than one task, making your work more efficient and the PowerShell program easier to work with.

With this multitasking, you are able to work with some of the jobs that take longer on a thread in the background, while still being able to use the shell for any of the other tasks that you would like. Then, once the job is complete, you are able to go through and retrieve the results that you want to form it. Now, there are a few different methods that you are able to use to make all of this happen, and they will include:

1. **Use the parameter of As Job from Get-WmlObject.** This is going to help you to create a new job, and the default name that comes with it will be something like Job1.

2. **You can also work with the Start-Job cmdlet.** This one is going to help you out because it lets you specify the name of a job, and then allows the programmer to create a job that is going to run one or more local scripts or commands as needed.

3. **Use the -AdJob parameter from the Invoke-Command.** This one is going to help with your remote commands because they are going to be on one of the threads in the background. The -JobName parameter is going to let you specify a custom job name if it is desired.

When you go through and create one of these new jobs that you will be using remember that you are always starting out by creating a single top-level master job, and then there have to be one or more of the child jobs. For jobs that are going to connect with more than one computer, you will need to set up a child job on each of those computers.

The Start-Job only part is going to be able to help you to start up a job that will run on your local computer. This doesn't mean that the commands that happen within that job are not able to connect with some of the other computers as well. Let's look at the command that you would use to make this happen:

Start-Job -command (Get-Service -computername server1, server2)

In this case, it can be more efficient to use remoting in order to get the workload distributed and to communicate over your own WinRM, of course, this assumes that we are already going to have the remoting enabled as we did in the past chapter. Now we want to stop and compare the code that we just did above with the following command:

Invoke-Command -command (Get-Service) -computername server1, server2 -asjob.

Here, the remote computers are set up in a manner that they are going to be able to run the command of Get-Service, and then they are going to return their results to you. And all of this is going to be done over the single port that is needed by WinRM. While this chapter is not really going to focus that much on the process of remoting, this brief illustration can help us to get the ideas that come with this one.

You can also choose to run the command of Get-Job to see a lot of information. This kind of information is going to include what jobs are currently defined, which ones are running, and which ones are completed along with some other information. Then you can work on the command for Stop-Job in order to kill any of the jobs that seem stuck and won't process on like they are supposed to. And Remove-Job is the command that you want to make sure that a job is deleted, as well as any of the results that it is storing in the memory.

To continue on with this idea, the programmer can work with the command of Wait-Job to cause the shell to pause until it has been able to complete a specific job. This is going to be useful inside of a script if you would like to start a job and then have the script wait a bit to get it all finished. All of these cmdlets for the jobs are going to accept a variety of parameters like -name or -ld so that you can go through and specify out which of the jobs that you would like to be able to manage.

There are a few tricks that we are able to use to help us get this part done. One of them is as follows. Let's say that you have a job, which we are going to name as Job1 that is going to be able to connect back to four computers. It is going to contain a child job, one that goes with each of the computers that you have. To see these, you can run the following code:

Get-Job -name Job1 | Format-List ∗

You will see that the property that is going to be able to list the names of these child jobs, which could be something like Job2, Job3, Job4, and Job5. You can use these job names to help you manage just one of the child jobs that you set up. Note that the master job is going to only show that it is completed for the status once all of the child jobs are done. So if there is a failure with just one of these child jobs, or one is taking more time than the others, then this means that the master job is not going to get done when you expect or it won't be able to finish at all. This is why it is important to know how many child jobs you have, and for you to go through and check on each one individually as well when something in the code is not working well.

When there are some results present for the job that you are doing, you can get to them by using the cmdlet for Receive-Job. Receiving the results for one of the master jobs that you have is going to take all of the results that you have for the child jobs. It is possible to also go through and specify the name or the job that you want if you would just like to look at the results for one of the child jobs that you are using.

The results are going to be buffered by the memory, only until they can be received by you. Once you are able to run the Receive-Job, by default, that memory buffer is going to become empty. This is why you want to make sure that you store your results in a file, a variable, or another place if you would like to be able to see some of these results at a later time. the best way to do this is to use the code below:

$results = Receive-Job -name Job2

In addition, you can choose to add in the parameter of -keep if you would like. This one is going to force our shell to leave a copy of the results in the buffer for the memory to get later. You do need to go through and add in some coding to make this happen though, and that coding is going to include the following syntax:

Receive-Job -name Job3 -keep

Finally, we need to make sure that we remember that the jobs we are working with here are actually going to be considered one of the extensibility points of PowerShell. This means that other developers are able to write some of the cmdlets that are going to create a variety of jobs. They may behave in a different manner, or even be used by the program differently. What we have spent time working on here is how to work with the built-in job mechanism that is provided through Microsoft.

Another thing that we need to remember here is that the My PowerShell home page is going to offer us to a lot of the articles and information that we need to know about PowerShell and how to use it. Looking through that page and some of the information that is present, there will ensure that you are able to get the most out of the coding that you do in this language.

Working with multitasking, which is sometimes going to be known as multithreading as well, is one of the best tasks that you are able to do when it comes to working in PowerShell. While some of the older versions of PowerShell did not add this feature, it really slowed down the system and if you were doing something that could take a long time, you just had to sit back and wait until it was all done and loaded and ready to use before you were able to add it or work with some of the other coding that you wanted to do.

As you can imagine, this is going to be frustrating for a lot of people and can make it difficult to do some of the coding that you would like to do. This can slow down your process, and it is going to make things frustrating as you go through and try to hurry things along. The good news is that some of the newer versions of PowerShell have fixed this problem, and will allow you to work on more task than one at the same time. This ensures that you are able to have one task going on in the background, and it takes a long time to finish, you can push it back to a background thread while working on the shell and anything else that you are able to do at that time.

This makes it a lot easier to work on some of the programming's that you would like, can make your coding more efficient, and ensures that you are not going to get stuck when you are waiting for a program to finish loading or for some other kind of task to get done. And in this chapter, we spent some time looking at the different parts that come with the code, ad all of the information that you need to really see why multitasking functions are important, and how to make them work for your needs.

Conclusion

Thank for making it through to the end of *PowerShell*, let's hope it was informative and able to provide you with all of the tools you need to achieve your goals whatever they may be.

The next step is to work on getting this program started and ready to go. We have already taken the time to talk about how PowerShell can work and some of the benefits of choosing this kind of coding language over some of the others. And if you are already working on a Windows computer and operating system, then it is going to be really easy for you to learn how to use this system without even having to take the time to download it to your computer.

We spent some time in this guidebook exploring what PowerShell is all about, how to write out some of your own codes in PowerShell, and the different actions that you are able to take to make this coding language work for your needs. And if you have ever looked at any of the other coding languages, or even tried to do them for yourself, you are going to be pleasantly surprised at how easy the PowerShell codes are going to be compared to some of those other coding languages.

When you are ready to learn more about what the PowerShell coding language can do for you, and how easy this whole process of coding can really be with the right tools, make sure to check out this guidebook to learn more about the wonderful world of PowerShell.

Finally, if you found this book useful in any way, a review on Amazon is always appreciated!

www.ingramcontent.com/pod-product-compliance
Lightning Source LLC
Chambersburg PA
CBHW070855070326
40690CB00009B/1856